Getting To Know...

Nature's Children

WILD HORSES

Martin Harbury

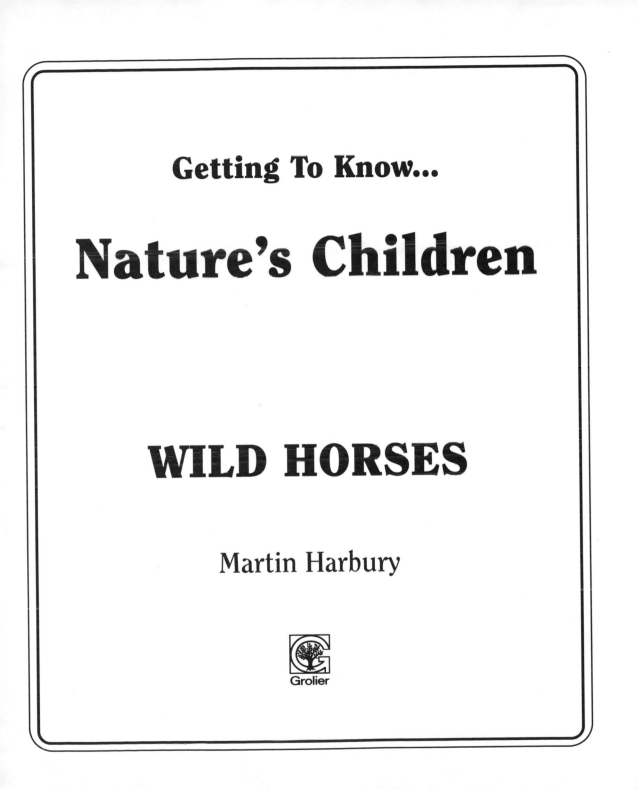

Grolier

Facts in Brief

Classification of North Amrican wild horses

    Class: *Mammalia* (mammals)
    Order: *Perissodactyla* (odd-toed hoofed mammals)
    Family: *Equidae* (horse family)
    Genus: *Equus*
    Species: *Equus caballus* (same species as the domestic horse)

Habitat. Forests, plains, deserts, mountains, and valleys.

Distinctive physical characteristics. Smaller than most domestic horses; usually has a stripe down the middle of the back, and dark stockings.

Habits. Lives in bands; is shy. Sometimes wild horses groom each other.

Diet. Grasses, shrubs, roots, and twigs.

Canadian Cataloguing in Publication Data

Harbury, Martin, 1945-
  Wild Horses

(Getting to know—nature's children)
Includes index.
ISBN 0-7172-1936-4

1. Wild horses—Juvenile literature.
I. Title. II. Series.

QL737.U62H37 1985   j599.72'5   C85-098743-1

Have you ever wondered . . .

When you think of horses, what do you think of? Do you think of:

- beautiful, long-legged race horses
- strong, plodding cart horses
- well-trained police horses
- gentle saddle ponies
- stubborn mules and asses?

Or do you think of wild horses?

People have always been fascinated by horses. They have written books about them, such as *Black Beauty* and *My Friend Flicka*, and made films about them, such as "The Black Stallion." Perhaps the most interesting of all the horses, though, is the wild horse.

There are bands of wild horses, sometimes called mustangs, in many places around North America. Perhaps, if you are lucky, you may some day see one of these mustang bands. But if you do, it will almost surely be from a distance, because wild horses are very shy and do not let people get close. If they sense people nearby, they run like the wind. In the blink of an eye they are gone.

Opposite page:

Home on the range.

The Horse Family History

If wild horses held a family picnic, it would be a strange gathering. There would be lots of close cousins—zebras, mules, asses, and every kind of saddle, race and cart horse. But that is not all. The wild horse's more distant cousins include the rhinoceros and the tapir!

Horses have been around since the time of the dinosaurs. One of their earliest ancestors, called Eohippus, did not look much like today's horses. It was tiny—about the size of a fox. Being small made it easier for Eohippus to escape huge dinosaurs by scampering under bushes. Another difference between today's horses and Eohippus was its feet. Instead of hoofs, Eohippus had pads with several toes.

Although the dinosaurs died out, probably because they were unable to adapt when the weather changed, the horse family did not. Instead, horses changed and grew until they looked like the horses we see today.

Once all horses were wild. But then people began to trap them and tame them. Now there are only a few wild horses left.

Horses in North America

The story of all North American horses is a long and interesting one. Long, long ago, horses lived in the wild in most parts of North America. But between 8000 and 10,000 years ago they all died out. Then there were no horses until the Spanish explorers brought some with them from Europe about 400 years ago.

Other Europeans who followed brought more horses, and soon the Indians started to use them too. Many of the horses escaped onto the prairies where the climate and the grass suited them well. The name mustang comes from a Spanish word which meant strayed or wild. Before long, thousands of mustangs were running free, quickly becoming more and more like their wild ancestors.

All North American wild horses, including this Assoteague Pony, are descended from domestic horses and are often referred to as feral rather than wild. The only true wild horse is the Przewalski, which once ranged in the area of the China-Mongolia border. It is extinct in its original habitat, but can be found in zoos and reserves around the world.

Where to Look for Wild Horses

The largest number of mustang bands live in
the deserts of Nevada. Deserts are not where
they prefer to live, but our cities and farms do
not leave them much choice. Fortunately, wild
horses are adaptable. They manage to survive
on sagebrush and other desert food and trickles
of water at a few water holes and springs.

Some other groups of wild horses live in the
Pryor Mountains of Montana and Wyoming.
The canyons and rivers, forests and meadows
of these beautiful mountains provide all the
mustangs' favorite foods. And they offer
plenty of places to hide.

Pryor Mountain mustangs are very shy. But
they are also very curious. If you tried to creep
up on a group of them to take a closer look,
you would probably soon lose sight of them.
Suddenly, you might feel as if *you* were being
watched. Often the curious Pryor Mountain
mustangs turn the tables on people by
sneaking around to follow them from behind.
But as soon as they are spotted they melt back
into the bushes and disappear!

The Sable Islanders

Sable Island is a large, sandy island that rises out of the Atlantic Ocean, off Canada's Nova Scotia coast. This is an unlikely place to find anything but gulls, sand dunes and fish. But there are all kinds of unlikely things on Sable Island.

Gray Seals breed there, and Ipswich Sparrows fly from as far as Georgia to lay their eggs there. Hundreds of shipwrecks litter the shores, and a few people live there to look after the lighthouses and the weather station. But the strangest thing about Sable Island is that 300 wild horses live there!

In fact, the tough little Sable Island horses have been there for hundreds of years. No one really knows how they got there, but some people think the first ones were survivors that swam ashore after a shipwreck.

A Sable Island wild horse may be small, but it is strong and hardy.

Winter Storms, Summer Playground

Life is not easy for the wild horses of Sable Island, especially in winter, when ferocious storms bring stinging ice and snow and chilling winds. Then, the little horses huddle behind the sand dunes for shelter. They grow long thick coats to keep out the cold. Sometimes, they have to break through ice to drink, or dig through the snow and sand to find hidden grass shoots.

But in the summer, when the sun's warmth beams down, they shed their long, woolly winter coats. Food is plentiful. The green grass grows fresh again and the ponds fill up with water. Then, the carefree Sable Island horses spend their days munching on sweet grass and running on the long, beautiful beaches.

Weathering the storm.

Small Cousins

Wild horses are smaller than most of their domestic cousins. This is because the food they eat in the wild is not as nutritious as the special foods and hay that people feed to domestic horses. A wild horse baby, or foal, which is caught very young and fed domestic foods will grow at least a hand taller than either of its parents. A hand is the unit that is used to measure the height of a horse. It is the width of the average adult man's hand—10 centimetres (4 inches).

Much of the difference in height between a wild horse and a domestic horse is in the foreleg. This works out very well for the wild horse because shorter bones are stronger. Thanks to its short, strong bones, a wild horse is less likely to break a leg if one of its hoofs slips into a hole.

Most wild horses are only between 12 and 14 hands at the shoulders, or between 122 and 142 centimetres (48 and 56 inches) tall. However, Sable Island horses are considerably smaller than this.

Opposite page:

This foal is definitely "a horse of a different color."

Coats of Many Colors

Wild horses come in a variety of colors—some are black, others are brown or white, and still others are in between.

Over many years, as horses lived in the wild, they began to have special markings, including a dark stripe down the back from the mane to the tail and dark lower legs. Sometimes, like their zebra cousins, wild horses might have little dark stripes called fingermarks on their upper legs. These markings help them blend in with their surroundings and make it more difficult for their animal enemies or people to see them. This is called camouflage.

Long ago different Indian tribes favored horses with certain markings. The Cheyenne, for example, liked Medicine Hat horses. These horses had white coats with special, darker markings on their heads and chests. The Cheyenne believed that these markings, which looked a bit like a war bonnet and a chest shield, helped protect both horse and rider.

The black markings on this foal's legs are referred to as its stockings.

Protective Hair

Horses that live in cold climates grow a thick winter coat every autumn and do not shed this hair until spring. The mane and tail hairs, however, are never shed.

In spring and summer, when there are lots of pesky bugs around, the horse uses its tail as a fly swatter to swish them away. If that does not work, it has special muscles under its skin that it can twitch to get rid of the insect pest.

Scratch and Clean

Horses love to groom themselves, and they have some unusual ways of keeping their coats clean and their skin free from itches. One favorite way is to roll on the ground on their backs. They will roll on the grass or in water or in a patch of dust or even in mud! If they find a really good back scratching spot, several horses may take turns rolling in it.

Horses also like to rub their heads and necks against fences, rocks or trees. Sometimes, they may scratch themselves with their hoofs or use their sharp front teeth.

You Scratch My Back . . .

Sometimes two horses will help each other groom spots that they cannot reach on their own. They use their teeth to nibble along each other's manes and necks and down the sides and back. They nibble and lick at all the places where there are tufts of matted hair or dead and itchy skin. Usually they start by standing face to face. Then they work their way along each other at the same time. When you see two horses grooming each other like this, you know that they are friends.

"A little more to the left please!"

Family Life

In the wild, horses live in family groups called bands. Every band is dominated by a powerful male horse, or stallion. The rest of the band is made up of female horses, or mares, and their young. The group of female horses in a band is called a harem.

Within the band, there is a strict ranking. The stallion is the leader. Next in importance is the stallion's mare. When the band moves, she leads. The other mares follow in order, and after them come the young horses.

Each horse knows its place in the order and is very careful to keep lower-ranking horses in their places. If one horse upsets the order, the others may use threatening movements of their heads and necks and lay their ears back against their heads to warn it to get back where it belongs. Sometimes, if a cheeky horse does not pay attention to these warnings, it may be bitten. If that does not work, a quick kick from two powerful back legs always works as a last resort!

Opposite page:

Banding together.

On the Watch

A horse's eyes are extraordinary. They are big, and the pupils can open very wide to take in any available light. This means they can see well at night, as well as in the daytime.

Your eyes are on the front of your head. Although you can see to the front and to the side, you cannot see things behind you. But a horse's eyes are toward the side of its head. So it can see things in front, to the side and even to the back of its head.

A horse's eyes are different from yours in another way too. They do not have to move in the same direction at the same time. Each eye moves independently. If you had eyes like a horse, you would be able to watch TV and look out of a window on the other side of the room at the same time! So do not be fooled. A horse that seems to be concentrating on eating is also completely aware of everything around, watching out for its neighbors or any approaching danger.

Opposite page:

Thirsty as it is, this horse will regularly pause and raise its head to check for danger.

What's That?

As well as good eyes, horses have very good hearing. Their pointed ears turn in almost any direction to catch sounds. If two horses cannot see each other, they will sometimes neigh to let each other know where they are.

Horses have super sniffers too. They can smell odors too faint for you to notice. If you watch them closely you will notice that they are always checking the air for scents.

With senses like these, and a close family group, it is no wonder that it is difficult to sneak up on wild horses. At the first sight, sound or smell of anything that might be dangerous, the stallion drives his band into a tight group and sends them galloping off to safety. He stays just at the rear, between his band and the threat.

Horse Talk

Like many animals, horses communicate with one another through the sounds they make. Horses whinny and neigh to each other. Usually this just means "I'm over here," but sometimes it can be a warning call.

But not all "horse talk" is done by whinnies and neighs. Horses can also send messages by the way they hold their ears. Ears flat back against the horse's head are usually saying: "Don't bother me. I'm angry." If a horse's ears are quickly perked forward it means it has been startled or frightened.

Horses usually graze in pairs or in small groups.

Chew, Chew, Chew

Fresh green grasses are the favorite food of all horses. But in some of the places they live, wild horses must make do with other plants or leaves. They have been known to eat holly leaves, gorse bushes, young twigs or to dig with their hoofs for plant roots. On Sable Island, the wild horses sometimes eat dry seaweed off the beaches in winter.

When they eat, horses crop the food off with their long, sharp front teeth and then grind it into a pulp with the flat back teeth called molars. Unlike cows and other grass-eating animals, horses have very inefficient stomachs and digestive systems. They need to chew their food until it is soft and mushy before they swallow it. Since they eat up to 14 kilograms (30 pounds) of grass a day, they sometimes spend half of their time just chewing!

Seaweed for lunch.

Running Shoes

If you spent a lot of time running over hard ground, you would want a sturdy pair of shoes to protect your feet. Horses have built-in shoes, called hoofs.

Overleaf:
Wild and free.

You may be surprised to learn that horses walk on tiptoes and that their hoofs are actually overgrown toenails. Over thousands and thousands of years, horses' feet changed from the padded feet with toes that Eohippus had. Gradually, horses began to walk on one long toe. On this toe the nail grew larger and flatter into a protective shoe, or hoof.

Horses that people ride need man-made horse shoes, because the extra weight they carry wears down their hoofs. But wild horses do not need extra shoes. Their own hoofed "running shoes" are enough protection.

"Catch me if you can!"

35

Like the Wind

When in danger, a wild horse's first thought is always to run away. All horses love to run, and they are perfectly suited to it. They have hoofs to protect their feet and long, powerful legs. Their wide, flaring nostrils can take in lots of air, and they have huge lungs to send oxygen where it is needed. All of these things make the horse one of the best and fastest runners in the world.

Of all horses, the thoroughbreds we see at racetracks are the fastest. Especially bred for speed, thoroughbreds have even longer legs than other horses. Over a few kilometres (a mile or two), they can outrun any horse.

But over long distances, a wild horse can outrun anything. It can run for hours on end, over country so rough that any other horse would probably slip or fall or just stop running. Because of this speed and endurance, the wild horse really has few natural enemies.

A Stallion Fight

Every spring, stallions and their mares mate.
When a mare is ready for mating, every
stallion in the neighborhood knows it because
she gives off a special scent. Very often several
stallions will try to mate with a mare, and her
family stallion will have to fight them off.

A stallion fight often looks much more
fierce than it really is. The two stallions prance
toward one another, with their necks arched.
They toss their heads and long manes from
side to side and stamp their hoofs on the
ground.

A stallion's flashing eyes and laid back ears,
its snorts and squeals are often enough to
make one horse retreat. If neither does, they
must fight. The two stallions rear up on their
hind legs and kick out with their front legs.
They try to knock each other over and to bite
each other's necks. Sometimes, if the fighting
is really fierce, they may suddenly wheel
around on their front legs and kick out with
their very powerful hind legs.

Usually, though, one stallion
gives up quite quickly. As soon as
it learns it is weaker it will turn
tail and run away. The proud
victor then prances back to his
harem and mates with his mare.

About 11 months after mating,
the mare will be ready to give
birth to a foal. This almost always
happens in the spring and almost
always at night. Darkness helps to
hide the young from predators.

A Foal is Born

Most of the time, a wild stallion tries to keep the mares in his harem close together, to protect them from danger. But in the spring, when a mare is ready to give birth, the stallion allows her to leave the group and to find a nearby sheltered spot.

At birth the foal is tiny and trembling. Immediately, its mother starts to lick it and nuzzle it, encouraging the delicate, spindly-legged baby to stand up. Normally, within an hour, the young colt or filly has stood up, wobbling, with legs splayed out, shaking from the effort.

Mares usually give birth to only one foal at a time.

Warm Welcome

At first, the new foal huddles close to its mother for warmth and comfort. But in just a few hours, after its first feeding, it will feel stronger and more confident. Then it is ready to meet the rest of the band. The adult horses seem to be curious about the new arrival. They sniff and lick it in welcome.

Very soon, the new foal is running and bouncing around, jumping and kicking up its heels, ready to gallop with the rest of the band. If there are other youngsters around, so much the better. The young foals will chase each other and play a kind of horse tag until they are exhausted or hungry and ready for another meal of mother's milk.

They quickly become stronger and soon are munching on grass as well as nursing on mother's milk. Chasing games now often end in playfights among young colts as they practice for the stallion fights they must one day join in.

Going It Alone

When they are about three years old, young stallions start to challenge their father. After a few challenges, the father becomes annoyed and chases the young stallion away. The time has come for it to fend for itself.

Very few young stallions are strong or smart enough to beat another stallion in a fight for a mare. Instead, they join up with other young stallions in a bachelor herd. Under the leadership of the strongest, they spend much of their time play-fighting, attempting raids on other bands to try and carry off a mare, and learning the skills they will need when they are ready to start their own families.

At about the same age, young females are also driven off by their father to find a mate. The young mare quickly finds male suitors. They may include a stallion who already has a small family, or perhaps a young leader of a bachelor herd. After a challenge, or perhaps a fight, the proud victor will come to claim his new mare and they will gallop off to new pastures, to start a new family.

Special Words

Band   A group of horses made up of a stallion, a harem of mares and young horses.

Camouflage   Colors or markings that help an animal blend in with its surroundings.

Colt   A young male horse.

Feral horses   Horses that roam wild in North America and in other parts of the world: France (Camargue horses); Britain, Iceland and Scandinavia (various pony species); and Australia (Brumbies). In some cases, populations shrank to the point that they were in danger of extinction, and the animals were moved to protected reserves. Examples are the Tarpans of Poland and the Assoteague Ponies on the islands off the coast of Maryland and Virginia.

Filly   A young female horse.

Foal   A baby horse.

Harem   The name for a group of mares in a band.

Hoofs   Hard nail-like growths that protect the horse's feet.

Lungs   The part of the body that takes oxygen from the air and makes it available to the rest of the body.

Mare   A female horse.

Mate   To come together to produce young.

Molars   Flat teeth at the back of the mouth that grind up food.

Mustangs   Wild horses, especially those that live in the deserts and mountains of the west.

Nurse   To drink milk from the mother's body.

Stallion   A male horse.

INDEX

Cover Photo: Zoe Lucas
Photo Credits: Ron Watts (First Light Associated Photographers), pages 4, 11, 19, 23, 24, 43, 44; Jamie Cruikshank (Miller Services), page 7; Michel Bourque (Valan Photos), pages 8, 31; Wambolt/Waterfield (Miller Services), page 12; Zoe Lucas, pages 15, 27, 28, 33, 34, 36-37, 41; United States Fish and Wildlife Service, page 16; K. Straiton (Miller Services), page 20.

Getting To Know...

Nature's Children

CARIBOU

Judy Ross

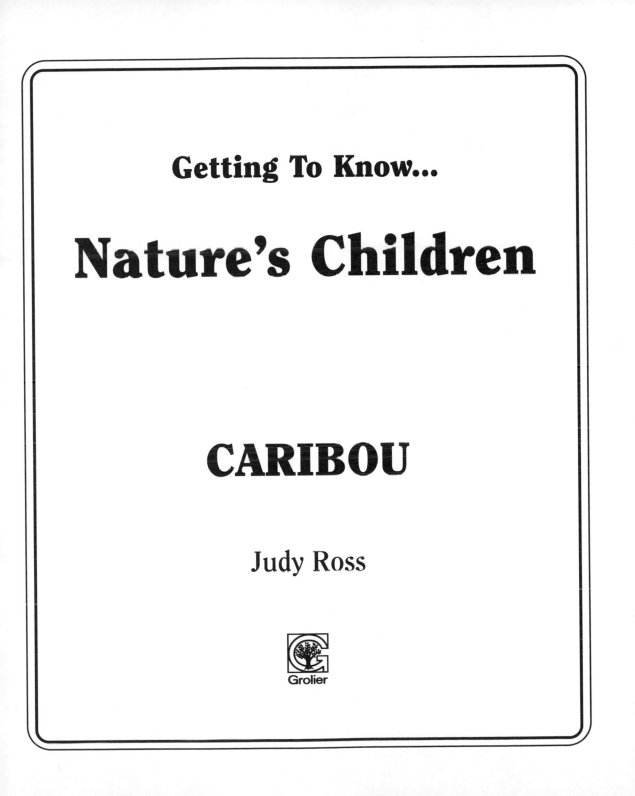

Grolier

Facts in Brief

Classification of the Caribou

Class: *Mammalia* (mammals)
Order: *Artiodactyla* (cloven-hoofed mammals)
Family: *Cervidae* (deer family)
Genus: *Rangifer*
Species: *Rangifer tarandus*

World distribution. Northern regions of North America, Europe, and Asia.

Habitat. Arctic tundra and/or coniferous forest.

Distinctive physical characteristics. Antlers on both males and females; small ears and tail; large feet; coloration varies with subspecies.

Habits. Lives in small bands or larger herds, depending on the time of year; is active during the day; barren-ground caribou migrate often and over great distances

Diet. Lichens, mushrooms, grasses, twigs, shrubs.

Canadian Cataloguing in Publication Data

Ross, Judy, 1942-
  Caribou

(Getting to know—nature's children)
Includes index.
ISBN 0-7172-1935-6

1. Caribou—Juvenile literature.
I. Title. II. Series.

QL737.U55R67 1985   j599.73'57   C85-098707-5

Have you ever wondered . . .

If you think that caribou look a lot like Santa's reindeer, you are right. Reindeer is the name given to caribou that live in Russia, Norway, Sweden and Finland. There, reindeer are raised as domestic animals, and many of them are really used for pulling sleds.

You might easily mistake a caribou for a very large deer. That is understandable, because the caribou is a member of the deer family. A baby caribou looks very much like a baby deer—except that it does not have white spots.

The antlers of the barren-ground caribou are larger than those of their woodland cousins.

Meet the Baby

This caribou baby, called a fawn, has already survived the most dangerous time in its young life—the first few hours after birth. Because it lives in a herd, it must be able to keep up with the group. If it gets left behind it could easily be caught by a wolf. This is why the mother caribou licks and nuzzles her newborn to encourage it to get up on its wobbly legs as soon as possible.

You were probably about one year old when you started walking. But this caribou fawn could stand up when it was only one hour old! In less than two hours, it was strong enough to walk several kilometres. Caribou fawns are fast as well as strong. A day-old fawn could run faster than a man!

Deer Relatives

The caribou is part of a very large family—the deer family. Some relatives that live in the caribou's neighborhood are the White-tailed Deer, the Mule Deer, the elk and the moose. All these deer relatives share certain features.

All of them have split hoofs, and none of them has any top front teeth. In addition, they are all cud chewers. This means they swallow food whole and store it in a special part of their stomach until they are ready to bring it back into their mouths and chew it.

But the most obvious similarity among deer family members is their antlers. All males grow and shed a new set of antlers every year. Unlike many of their deer relatives, the female caribou usually grows antlers too.

As a caribou's antlers grow, they are covered with a furry skin known as velvet.

Caribou Country

There are two kinds of caribou in North America. One kind lives in forests and mountains. These are called woodland caribou. The others, called the barren-ground caribou, live on the frozen tundra of the far north.

The woodland caribou does not live as far north as its cousin, but winters in its forest home can be cold too.

The barren-ground caribou live where the winters are long and harsh. The cold often lasts for nine months. During this time, the ground is covered with snow, and the rivers and lakes are frozen over.

Where caribou can be found in North America.

10

Keeping Warm

The caribou has many ways of keeping warm in winter.

It has a special double-thick fur coat to keep body heat in and the cold and wet out. The long outer guard hairs are hollow. They contain air, which provides some insulation, and they lie flat against the caribou's body to form a shield against rain and snow. Under the guard hairs is a thick crinkly underfur which traps the air warmed by the caribou's body.

You know how cold your nose can get on a winter day. The caribou is not bothered by a cold nose. Its nose is completely covered with hair. Every part of the caribou's body is furry, even its ears and tail. The caribou's ears and tail are tiny for such a big animal. That way less body heat is lost through them.

The coat of the caribou is longer and denser than that of other deer.

Changing Coats

You would not want to wear your winter coat all year long, would you? Of course not. In summer you would be too hot.

The caribou does not wear its thick coat all year long either. It sheds it in great clumps in the early summer. Although the caribou looks tattered and patchy during this molt, it is never bald. A new lightweight coat grows in as the old winter coat falls out.

Both the woodland and the barren-ground caribou are mostly brown, with white markings on their legs, belly, neck and tail. The woodland caribou are generally a dark chocolate brown, while the barren-ground caribou are a lighter, clove color.

Old bulls, like the one in the center of this picture can be identified by their white mane.

Fabulous Feet

The caribou's feet are well designed for walking in deep snow. Its large hoofs splay out as it walks to spread its body weight over a bigger surface—a little bit as snowshoes support a person's weight.

Ice is not a problem either. In winter the horny edge around the outside of the hoof grows. This helps the caribou dig its hoofs into ice, almost as if it was wearing cleats. At the same time, the pads in the center of the hoof shrink and become hard and horny. This way they are less likely to be cut by hardened snow and ice. And hair grows between the caribou's toes, forming a warm covering over the pad.

In summer the fleshy pads on the caribou's feet balloon up in size. This gives the caribou lots of support as it walks over soft, marshy ground.

There's nothing dainty about a caribou's feet!

Caribou hoofs.

Summer

Winter

17

Up Close

If a caribou were to stand beside its enormous relative, the moose, it would look pretty small. But an average male woodland caribou, called a buck, weighs about 225 kilograms (500 pounds). The female, or doe, is quite a bit smaller.

Barren-ground caribou are considerably smaller than their woodland cousins. An average buck weighs about 110 kilograms (240 pounds). That is half the weight of its cousin.

The size of the caribou depends on the area where it lives. In areas where there is plenty of food, the caribou are bigger. Where food is scarce, the caribou are smaller. Since it is more difficult to find food in the frozen north, it is not surprising that the barren-ground caribou are generally smaller.

Scratching these antlers is no easy task.

Handsome Headgear

Can you imagine carrying a couple of heavy thick branches on top of your head all day long? That probably would not bother a caribou. It is used to having a lot of weight on its head. A buck's thick antlers can grow to as long as one metre (3 feet) and weigh several kilograms.

Many females have antlers too, but they are much smaller, and reach full size when the doe is two or three years old. A buck's antlers continue to grow until he is between six and nine years old.

No two sets of caribou antlers are exactly the same. But if you look closely you will see that they are all made up of the same three parts. There are two long antlers which curve back from the forehead and up; a pair of brow tines which are smaller and curve out in front; and the shovel, which is the part that curves down over the caribou's nose.

Usually there is only one shovel but sometimes there are two. This part of the caribou's antlers probably got its name because people thought that caribou used it to shovel snow in winter when looking for food. We know now that this is not so. It uses its front hoofs to dig for food.

Caribou shed their antlers and grow new ones every year, but bucks and does follow different timetables. The bucks begin to shed their antlers in early November, although the younger ones sometimes keep theirs until as late as January. Does do not shed their antlers until the spring.

The buck's new antlers begin to grow in March. At first they are just fuzzy knobs. When antlers are growing in, they are covered with a soft, furry skin called velvet. This velvet contains blood vessels which nourish the antlers and help them grow. By mid-summer the buck's antlers stop growing, and the velvet begins to fall off. Caribou rub their antlers against trees and bushes to help get rid of this fuzzy coating.

Does grow their new set of antlers in summer, after their babies are born.

Caribou antlers.

Female

Male

Living Together

You will hardly ever see a caribou on its own. Caribou are sociable animals and live in small bands or large herds, depending on their type and the time of year.

The woodland caribou live in family bands that are usually made up of fewer than 50 animals. These bands change during the year. Sometimes males of the same age form a band and females another band. Usually it is only at mating season that bands of females and males join.

The barren-ground caribou live in large herds made up of thousands of animals.

On the Move

Some animals have homes in which they spend much of their lives. But not the caribou. They are wanderers, on the move most of the year. In the summer they move from pasture to pasture in search of food. In the fall, they head for well-forested areas where they can find protection from the cold and snow. And in spring they travel to special birthing grounds where the young are born.

Generally woodland caribou travel less than barren-ground caribou. The woodland animals often move deeper into the forests or down mountains in the fall, but it is their more northerly cousins who are the real wanderers.

The barren-ground caribou may travel up to 1300 kilometres (800 miles) between winter feeding grounds and summer birthing grounds. They have special routes which they use every year on these migrations.

If you ran as fast as you could you might keep up with walking caribou— until you ran out of breath.

A Noisy Brown Sea

People who have been lucky enough to see a large herd of barren-ground caribou migrating are amazed by the sight. They say it looks like a sea of animals passing by.

As they walk or run the caribou's legs make an odd clicking sound. This is caused when part of one leg rubs against another. On top of this clicking is the sound of antlers clashing. This clicking and clashing can sometimes be heard quite a distance away. And if there are young caribou fawns in the herd, another sound adds to the noise—loud bawling.

Caribou sometimes travel in single file, following a leader along a narrow path. Some herds are so large that it takes days for all the caribou to pass!

Follow the leader.

Running and Swimming

Sometimes a herd of caribou just pokes along, but if they are alarmed, they can gallop at speeds of up to 65 kilometres (40 miles) per hour. But even their normal walking speed is a lot faster than yours.

When migrating, caribou often have to cross wide rivers or lakes. This is no problem because they are strong swimmers. Their wide hoofs make good paddles, and their hollow, air-filled guard hairs act like a life jacket to help keep them afloat.

Caribou often cross lakes and rivers during their annual migration.

Curious Caribou

We all think of cats as being curious animals, but did you know caribou are curious too? They do not seem to be able to resist unusual sights, such as a man waving his arms. They will run off so that they are out of danger then turn and stare. Sometimes they will even come back for a closer look.

Even then, their curiosity may not be fully satisfied and they may try to move downwind of whatever it was that caught their attention. That is because they depend above all on their keen sense of smell to give them information about what is around them.

"Who are you?"

Finding Food

Caribou eat as they walk, browsing on willow shoots and nipping green buds off shrubs and leaves off plants. But the mainstay of their diet is lichen, a low-growing plant that clings to rocks and trees. The average barren-ground caribou can eat about four and a half kilograms (10 pounds) of lichen a day. For a real gourmet treat caribou eat mushrooms.

In winter, when the ground is covered in snow, the caribou eat the twigs of willow and birch trees or dig down with their hoofs to find frozen bits of plants beneath the snow. They rely on their strong sense of smell to find lichen and dried horsetails buried under the snow.

Sometimes in winter caribou even munch on muskrat dens. These are made of dried plants and grasses. Good food for a caribou, but what a surprise for the muskrat!

After feeding the caribou looks for a comfortable resting place and settles down to chew its cud.

Tear, Swallow, Grind

The caribou cannot bite off leaves or bits of lichen because it does not have any top front teeth. Instead it has a rough plate on the roof of its mouth, and it tears off pieces of food. In the back of its mouth are a set of flattened teeth called molars, perfect for grinding up tough plants.

The caribou does not chew its food right away. It swallows lichen, leaves and buds whole and stores them in one part of its stomach. Later it finds a nice spot to lie down. As it relaxes it brings the food, or cud, back to its mouth and grinds it up into a pulp. This is why caribou, like other deer, are called cud chewers.

Danger!

Grizzly Bears, lynx and wolverines will all attack caribou, but wolves are their main enemy. Groups of wolves often follow a herd of caribou, waiting to catch a calf or a sick or old member of the herd. Only occasionally will they catch a healthy adult. By keeping the caribou numbers down, the wolves are actually helping the herd. Since they take the weaker members, there is more food for the stronger ones, who are better able to survive.

When a caribou senses danger it lifts its head high with its ears pointing up and forward, raises its tail and holds one leg out to the side. This rather odd-looking pose warns other caribou "Watch out—danger is near!" If the caribou that has given the alarm suddenly starts to run off, all the others will run too, whether they have seen the enemy or not.

Sometimes a frightened caribou will rear up on its hind legs just like a horse. When it does this its hoofs spread apart and a special scent is deposited on the ground. Other caribou know that this smell means "Watch out!"

Opposite page:

An alert caribou often sniffs the air to check for any strange scent that might betray the presence of an enemy.

Pesky Pests

Wolves may be the biggest danger to the caribou, but flies and mosquitoes cause them the most bother. In the summer the ground where barren-ground caribou live is soggy, and there are many streams and ponds where black flies and mosquitoes breed. Being bitten is an annoying but inevitable way of life for northern animals.

Unfortunately the caribou's lightweight summer coat is not thick enough to protect it from bites. And its tail is not long enough to use as a fly swatter. All a caribou can do is snort with irritation and try to outrun these airborne pests. Sometimes caribou will wear themselves out trying to avoid being bitten.

When the insects are in full force, the caribou often climb up high hills or mountains to find a breezy spot with fewer bugs. If they are still being bothered, they will even plunge into freezing cold northern waters to escape.

On the run.

Mating Time

Caribou mate in October and early November.

A woodland buck gathers a harem of a dozen or more does. For the rest of the mating season, he will spend much of his time rushing around trying to keep them together and fighting off any other buck that tries to get near them.

Barren-ground males do not gather harems. Instead they mate at random in their large herds.

Mating season is a time of great activity for the males of both caribou types. They duel with other males, bellow loudly and sometimes even thrash their antlers around in a thicket of bushes. Before mating season caribou bucks are fat and sleek looking. But they lose weight during the mating season because they do not have much time to eat. When winter comes they are often tired and tattered looking.

Head to head combat.

New Life in Spring

After the long cold winter, spring is very welcome in caribou country. The days are getting longer and warmer, and the does are almost ready to give birth.

Most caribou have special birthing grounds where they go to have their young. If she is traveling with a herd, the mother simply drops behind the group when it is time to have her fawn.

The fawns are born in mid-May to early June. Usually just one fawn is born, but occasionally there may be two or three. The fawn is long legged and reddish brown in color. It weighs about four and a half to six kilograms (10 to 13 pounds). That is about as much as a medium-sized dog.

The mother is very protective. She licks and cleans her baby and cuddles and nudges it constantly. When it has rested, she gently shoves it so that it will stand up and start walking.

The young fawn seems to be all legs!

A Fine Fawn

The fawn's hind legs look very wobbly and bent at first, but soon they straighten out. Before long it can keep up with its mother and the rest of its band or herd. And it can swim too!

Like most babies, fawns love to explore and meet other youngsters. Sometimes one will wander away and get lost. Then the mother goes after her fawn. She can tell it from a group of other look-alike fawns by its scent.

These active babies grow so fast that they double their birth weight in just 10 days. They begin to graze on a few choice bits of greenery after about two weeks, but continue to drink their mother's milk for at least a month. If the weather is very harsh the mother will continue to nurse her fawn for a longer period.

Caribou fawns sprout antlers during their first autumn.

On the Move Again

Often mother caribou with fawns of the same age gather together in a band. That way they can set a speed that the fawns can keep up with.

By fall the fawn will be about five months old and starting to grow its first set of antlers. Soon its mother will be getting ready to mate again. And it will be time to move to more sheltered winter areas.

The fawn will probably stay with its mother through the winter but will go off with other year-old fawns when the new group of babies are born in the spring.

Few caribou live to be older than four or five in the wild. While that might seem like a very short life to us, it is time for a caribou to have several young of its own and walk thousands of kilometres (miles) in its never-ending wanderings.

Special Words

Buck   Male caribou.

Cud   Hastily swallowed food brought back for chewing by cud chewers such as cows and caribou.

Doe   Female caribou.

Fawn   Young caribou.

Guard hairs   Long coarse hairs that make up the outer layer of a caribou's coat.

Harem   Group of does that a buck gathers together at mating time.

Hoofs   Feet of caribou, deer, cattle and some other animals.

Lichen   A flowerless moss-like plant that grows on rocks and trees.

Mate   To come together to produce young.

Migrate   To travel regularly in search of feeding or birthing grounds.

Molt   To shed fur and grow new fur, usually at a change of seasons.

Nurse   To drink milk from a mother's body.

Tine   Prong of a caribou's antlers.

Tundra   Flat land in the arctic where no trees grow.

Velvet   Soft skin that covers a caribou's antlers while they grow.

INDEX

Cover Photo: Brian Milne (First Light Associated Photographers)
Photo Credits: Stephen J. Krasemann (Valan Photos), pages 4, 8, 11, 15, 19, 22, 25, 30, 34, 37, 38; Fred Bruemmer, page 7; J.D. Taylor (Miller Services), pages 13, 33, 41; J.D. Markou (Miller Services), page 16; Mike Beedele (Miller Services), page 26; Patrick Morrow (First Light Associated Photographers), page 29; Wayne Lankinen (Valan Photos), pages 42, 45.